100 INSPIRING AND RELATABLE QUOTES

QUOTES FROM THE BOTTOM OF THE HEART

NISHA NANDHINI S

Dedicated to my lovable and ever supporting parents

Mr. R. Shankar

&

Mrs. S. Geetha

Contents

About The Author

Ms. Nisha Nandhini S is an aspiring botany student, pursuing her bachelor's degree in Bishop Heber College, Trichy. She was a summer research fellow at Central Salt and Marine Research Institute, Bhavnagar, Gujarat for 2 months. She is a bibliophile, reading inspired writer and wishes to create ripples in the society with the tip of her pen. She has a confident personality and serving mind. Her goal is to increase the green cover and conserve mother nature and her creations.

Acknowledgements

The author would like to thank her family for their extreme support in all kinds of situations. Her parents have been a constant source of motivation to her. She also likes to express her gratitute to her sister and brother for their encouragement.

Preface

In this book, the author had expressed her thoughts in the form of quotes. These quotes were inspired either from her everyday life or from the experiences encountered by her friends and family. Several of her friends found these quotes to be more relatable to their life. This encouraged her to pen down this book.

1. SUCCESS

(1)

Every path may not lead to success but teach something that takes you closer to success.

(2)

First step of success is to make your body do what your mind says.

(3)

There can be no best friends like dedication and hard work, when they join together anything can be achieved.

(4)

Reading books about success without action is futile.

(5)

Dare to stand first, winning or losing you will have a place in history.

2. FAILURE

(6)

If success can open a way, failure can open million ways.

(7)

People who laugh at our failures, haven't even tried, so stop
worrying about them.

(8)

If you cannot gather the strength to face failure, don't dare to try.

(9)

Conqueror of fear of failure will soon become the ruler of success.

(10)

When you fail, sit back, relax.
Ponder over and start again

3. LIFE

(11)

Never let your curiosity die without it life is nothing.

(12)

If you cannot find the purpose of your life, create one.

(13)

Life takes you through crests and troughs to teach the rights and wrongs.

(14)

Learn to motivate yourself because the one who is ready to do it today may not do it tomorrow.

(15)

Life can give you more than your wish and also take away more than you guess.

4. OPPORTUNITIES

(16)

Opportunities are everywhere; all you need is an optimistic mind.

(17)

When everyone is busy searching for opportunities, be the one who creates them.

(18)

Even if you get a small chance make the best out of it.

(19)

Subway surfers taught one thing, you cannot travel in the same path for quite long time. Take diversions and explore new opportunities.

(20)

Life is all about success and if you fail it is about the next success.

5. LONELINESS

(21)

Learning to console yourself makes you emotionally stronger and bolder.

(22)

Dare to take lonely paths it will take you to unexplored destinations.

(23)

When my brain said, "I have nobody".
My heart said. "Excuse me! I am beating for you."

(24)

Loneliness isn't a pain, it is a medicine to several kinds of pain.

(25)

Enjoy people's company long till it lasts and enjoy your own company when it is lost.

6. BEAUTY

(26)

Real beauty isn't something that is felt by eyes but felt by heart.

(27)

Everybody is beautiful but only some eyes can feel it.

(28)

Take efforts to look beautiful not just in mirror but also in minds of people.

(29)

Being benevolent makes you a beautiful person.

(30)

Rich dress doesn't make you beautiful but rich character can.

7. EMOTIONS

(31)

If you cannot be emotionally strong, at least try to act like being one.

(32)

Emotions are safe until they stay within you. Protect your emotions to avoid being influenced by others.

(33)

Accept the way you are, so that nobody's rejection can hurt you.

(34)

In a world where people hurt, be the one who heals.

(35)

Keep yourself busy such that deleted messages and blocked contacts bother you the least.

8. LOVE

(36)

Be a one who loves chocolate more than cover of the chocolate.

(37)

Love is like a bird, never cage it!
Let it fly, if it is true it will come back to you.

(38)

If someone really loves you, they will give you the
most special and costly gift which none can buy you, its their
TIME!

(39)

Addiction to humans is more dangerous than addiction to drugs,
there are no de-addiction centres available.

(40)

If you need lies to maintain love, it isn't love anymore.

9. SELF WORTH

(41)

Whatever be the situation, make yourself first in your priority list.

(42)

Best invention anyone can do is to bring the best out of themselves.

(43)

You may be zero but you are responsible to add a number before and make yourself valuable.

(44)

The day you understand your worth is the day you started to live.

(45)

Never set limits based on what others say about you, discover yourself and then set your limits.

10. TIME

(46)

Stop wasting time arguing with fools, start investing them for your future.

(47)

When you are hurt, it isn't time to breakdown, it is the time when you should build up.

(48)

Be like a watch, don't watch anyone move fast and forward.

(49)

Time is the only investment that will surely yield you greater profit in future.

(50)

Enlarge your vision, examine before performing and execute at the right time.

11. HAPPINESS AND SADNESS

(51)

If you cannot make others happy, try making yourself happy at least.

(52)

Inability to cry when you wish to do so worsens the pain.

(53)

Smile is the cheapest ornament but not everyone can buy it.

(54)

Sadness is shared not just with diaries but also with pillows and bed sheets.

(55)

As long as your lips can smile, nothing can make you fail.

12. TRUTH AND LIE

(56)

A building built with lies cannot withstand a gentle breeze of truth.

(57)

Trusting is important but knowing whom to trust is even more important.

(58)

When someone whom you trust leaves you,
clutch hands of passion, they will unveil a new world.

(59)

Learn to be alone because it is eternal.

(60)

Everybody will leave you, when is the mysterious question!

13. RELATIONS

(61)

One who was with you when you had nothing is one who deserves everything of you.

(62)

Dad is the king a girl's world; he rules it with utmost strictness ad cares with the purest love.

(63)

World is big enough to find new friends but very small to move away from old ones.

(64)

Life with one who is fond of you is more beautiful than with one whom you are fond of.

(65)

Never ignore your parents, without them your present state is unimaginable.

14. CONTRAST

(66)

Argue with only ones who are ready to listen you.

(67)

Not just gods and angels, even elections can do miracles.

(68)

A place where promises before love and election are fulfilled is the happiest one.

(69)

If you can channelize every little positivity you have, you can easily swim through an ocean of negativity.

(70)

The need of god ends where human needs are satisfied but the interesting part is that human needs are insatiable.

15. ATTITUDE

(71)

Attitude is staying away from attitude less people.

(72)

After taking up a job, Do or never die until it's done.

(73)

Don't search for a kingdom to rule, create a kingdom and rule.

(74)

Judge me by talking to me not with what others said about me.

(75)

People don't leave, they understand that they are not worth to be with you and maintain their distance.

16. MATERIALISTIC THINGS

(76)

A lap to rest on is much better than having lakhs to spend.

(77)

Life is best without addiction to materialistic things.

(78)

Always remember that money isn't the only need, it is just one of several needs.

(79)

In the search of materialistic things, we are losing several valuable relationships.

(80)

Think about foodless people when you think your food is tasteless

17. PROBLEMS AND PAINS

(81)

Best advices are heard from the most broken hearts

(82)

Traitors make our boring life a bit more interesting.

(83)

When you face problems remember that life is a brakeless car, you cannot stop instead you have to find an alternate path.

(84)

Being alone is the best way to avoid hurting and being hurt.

(85)

Every problem is easy to solve, if you are ready to change your perception.

18. SELF RESPECT

(86)

Every relationship is important but never at the cost of self respect.

(87)

When you do your best you need not bow your head.

(88)

Self respect is one of basic needs like food and water.

(89)

If people call your self respect as ego, it is their mistake and never yours.

(90)

Your self respect should be very high such that none should ever think of buying it.

19. GOAL

(91)

Never let your capabilities become prisoner of your fear.

(92)

Never advertise your goals, let your results speak.

(93)

Imperfect past does not matter, long you have the confidence to create a perfect future.

(94)

Destination is reached not by daydreamers but by determined people.

(95)

Path led by passion and dedication can never go wrong.

20. BEING YOURSELF

(96)

Learn from everyone but never mimic anyone.

(97)

Don't lose yourself in an attempt to satisfy someone.

(98)

As long as your actions do not influence others you need not explain them.

(99)

Even when everybody hates you, make sure that your love for yourself never fades.

(100)

If you being yourself is problem to someone, better stay away from them.

Thank you for spending time with the pages of the book!